Amazing ANIMAL Groups

A Fun Exploration of Nature

Niki Mitchell

Have you ever heard of a "tower" of giraffes? Or a "zeal" of zebras? These are just a few examples of the unique names given to groups of animals. In this book, we will connect names and explore fascinating facts along the way!

Crocodile Floats and Their Cold-Blooded Ways

Crocodiles are cold-blooded reptiles and live in tropical regions around the world. Did you know that a group of crocodiles is called a "float"? Typically, these groups are situated close to water bodies, basking in the sun. But don't get too close, as crocodiles are notorious for their deadly bites!

A Float of Crocodiles

Elephant Parades and Their Amazing Trunks

Elephants are one of the largest land animals found in Asia and Africa. Elephants are herbivores and can eat up to three hundred pounds of food a day! A group of elephants is called a "parade"—and with their strong trunks and intelligent minds, they truly are a sight to see.

A Parade of Elephants

Flamboyance of Flamingos and

Their Beautiful Pink Feathers

Flamingos have long legs, pink feathers, and unique beaks. You will find these birds near bodies of water in South America, Africa, and southern Asia. A group of flamingos is called a "flamboyance"—a fitting name for these striking birds who use their feathers to communicate with each other.

A Flamboyance of Flamingos

Giraffe Towers

and Their Long Necks

Giraffes hold the title for the tallest mammal in the world. These gentle creatures have tough and long tongues, perfect for grabbing leaves! They can be found in Africa, roaming the savannas and woodlands. A group of giraffes is called a "tower"—a name that reflects their height and elegance.

A Tower of Giraffes

Hippopotamus Bloats and Life by the Water's Edge

Hippopotamuses may look cute and cuddly, but they are actually one of the most dangerous animals in Africa. These herbivores have strong jaws and an aggressive behavior. A group of hippopotamuses is called a "bloat"—a term that accurately describes their round and bloated appearance.

A Bloat of Hippopotamuses

Hyena Cackles and Their Hunting Tactics

Hyenas are recognized for their distinct laughter-like cries. In Africa and Asia, these carnivorous animals with sharp teeth and strong jaws hunt in packs. A group of hyenas is called a "cackle"—a fitting name for these vocal animals.

A Cackle of Hyenas

Jaguar Shadows and Their Stealthy Ways

Jaguars, the largest cats in the Americas, are elusive and powerful big cats that prowl the rainforests in Mexico and South America. They have stunning black and gold spotted coats and stealthy hunting tactics. A group of jaguars is called a "shadow"—a name that perfectly captures their elusive nature.

A Shadow of Jaguars

Kangaroo Troops and Their Pouches

Kangaroos are unique marsupials that hop around the Australian Outback. They are known for their powerful legs and their ability to carry their babies (called joeys) in their special pouches. A group of kangaroos is called a "troop"—a term that reflects their social nature.

A Troop of Kangaroos

Leopard Leaps

and Their Camouflage

Leopards are renowned for their beautiful spotted coats and their ability to blend into their surroundings. The sleek and powerful cats gracefully climb trees, stealthily stalk their prey, and prefer to spend most of their time alone. These carnivores inhabit Africa and Asia. A group of leopards, comprising of a mother and her cubs, is called a "leap"—a name that reflects their agility and speed.

A Leap of Leopards

Owl Parliaments and Their Nocturnal Habits

Owls are birds of prey that are known for their gigantic eyes and hoots. Because of their silent flight and keen eyesight, they are remarkable hunters. Wisdom is often associated with these nocturnal animals found worldwide. A group of owls, comprising of up to a hundred birds, is called a "parliament"—a term that reflects their perceived intelligence.

A Parliament of Owls

Parrot Pandemonium and Their Colorful Feathers

Parrots have the ability to mimic human speech. They can learn many words and even have unique personalities! You can find these birds in tropical regions all over the world. A group is known as "pandemonium"—a fitting name for a group of birds that love to chatter.

A Pandemonium of Parrots

Porcupine Prickles and Their Protective Quills

Porcupines are slow-moving herbivores found in North and South America, Africa, and Asia. While they have sharp quills that help protect them from predators, they are gentle natured. A group of porcupines is called a "prickle"—a name that reflects their spiky appearance.

A Prickle of Porcupines

Rhinoceros Crashes

and Their Horns

Rhinoceroses are large herbivores that live in Africa and Asia. They are recognized for their protective features, such as their thick hide and their iconic single or double horn on their noses. They have poor eyesight but a keen sense of smell. A group of rhinoceroses, which can consist of up to fourteen, is called a "crash"—a name that reflects their powerful nature.

A Crash of Rhinocerouses

Skunk Stenches and Their Odor

Skunks are known for their distinctive black and white stripes and their ability to release a strong scent when threatened. These animals inhabit North and South America. Skunks are very solitary animals and prefer to spend most of their time alone. A group of skunks, comprising of a mother and her young, is called a "stench"—a term that accurately describes their potent smell.

A Stench of Skunks

Tiger Streaks and Their Stripes

Asia's dense jungles are home to the iconic tiger. They are known for their striking orange coats and black stripes. They are very territorial and communicate with each other through various sounds and body language. A group of tigers, which comprise of a mother and her cubs, is called a "streak"—a name that reflects their lightning-fast speed.

A Streak of Tigers

Vulture Venues and Their Scavenging Habits

Vultures are scavengers that play an essential role in keeping the environment clean by eating carcasses. They use their sense of smell to locate food and their sharp beaks for tearing apart their meals. These birds are worldwide and frequently spotted circling over carrion. The term "venue" is used for a group of up to one hundred vultures, reflecting their habit of gathering in one place.

A Venue of Vultures

Zebra Zeal and

Their Striped Coats

The distinctive black and white striped coats of zebras are coupled with their impressive ability to run up to speeds of thirty-five miles per hour. The savannas and grasslands of Africa are home to these herbivores. A group of zebras is called a "zeal"—a name that accurately reflects their energy and enthusiasm.

A Zeal of Zebras

Animal Groups Have Cool Names

All of these animals have unique group names—but they all share one thing in common. They are and amazing creatures. If you want to discover more animal facts, visit your local zoos, or check out the thousands of books found in libraries, bookstores, or online.

Vocabulary

Africa	hippopotamuses	rhinoceros
aggressive	hyena	savannas
aggressive	hyena	savannas
Asia	kangaroo	scavengers
Australian	leaps	shadow
bloats	leopard	skunk
cackles	Mexico	solitary
carnivorous	mimic	South America
cold-blooded	nocturnal	stenches
communicate	owl	streaks
crashes	pandemonium	territorial
crocodile	parade	tiger
elephant	parliament	tower
flamboyance	parrot	troops
flamingos	porcupine	venue
float	predators	vulture
giraffe	prickles	zeal
herbivores	protective	zebra

About the Author

I was born in Chicago, Illinois, and moved to Whittier, California in first grade. With a houseful of books and a library located a few short blocks away, my love of reading began at a young age. My soft spot for animals comes from growing up with dogs, parakeets, turtles, chickens, ducks, and other critters. Over thirty years of teaching has given me insight into children's thinking and the skills they need to read independently. If you enjoyed this story, feedback on Facebook or Amazon would be greatly appreciated.

I look forward to hearing from my readers.

Love,

Niki Mitchell

Website: https://kuriouskatz.weebly.com/

Facebook: Kurious Katz Author Page

https://www.facebook.com/kuriouskatzauthor/

TikTok: @kuriouskatzbooks

Books by Niki Mitchell can be read in any order.

PRECIOUS PUPS: BREEZY GETS ADOPTED
FOSTER CATS: ARTEMIS AND HER SNEAKY BROTHER
KURIOUS KATZ
KURIOUS KATZ AND THE BIG MOV
KURIOUS KATZ AND THE NEW FRIEND
KURIOUS KATZ AND THE HALLOWEEN COSTUMES
KURIOUS KATZ AND THE PLAY DAY
KURIOUS KATZ AND THE BIRTHDAY PARTY
KURIOUS KATZ AND THE CHRISTMAS TREE
KURIOUS KATZ AND THE BEST CHRISTMAS EVER
KURIOUS KATZ AND THE SNOWY DAY
KURIOUS KATZ AND THE VALENTINE SURPRISE
KURIOUS KATZ AND THE FOURTH OF JULY
KURIOUS KATZ AND THE SNICKERDOODLE STORY